ANIMALS
That Make a Difference!

Bees

Ashley Lee &
Jared Siemens

Explore other books at:
WWW.ENGAGEBOOKS.COM

VANCOUVER, B.C.

e↗ WWW.ENGAGEBOOKS.COM

Bees: Level 1
Animals That Make a Difference!
Lee, Ashley 1995 –
Siemens, Jared 1989 –
Text © 2021 Engage Books

Edited by: A.R. Roumanis
and Lauren Dick

Text set in Arial Regular.
Chapter headings set in Arial Black.

FIRST EDITION / FIRST PRINTING

LIBRARY AND ARCHIVES CANADA CATALOGUING IN PUBLICATION

Title: Animals That Make a Difference: Bees Level 1
Names: Jared Siemens, author

Identifiers: Canadiana (print) 20200309064 | Canadiana (ebook) 20200309072
ISBN 978-1-77437-662-1 (hardcover)
ISBN 978-1-77437-663-8 (softcover)
ISBN 978-1-77437-664-5 (pdf)
ISBN 978-1-77437-665-2 (epub)
ISBN 978-1-77437-666-9 (kindle)

Subjects:
LCSH: Bees—Juvenile literature
LCSH: Human-animal relationships—Juvenile literature

Classification: LCC QL565.2 .S54 2020 | DDC J595.79/9—DC23

Contents

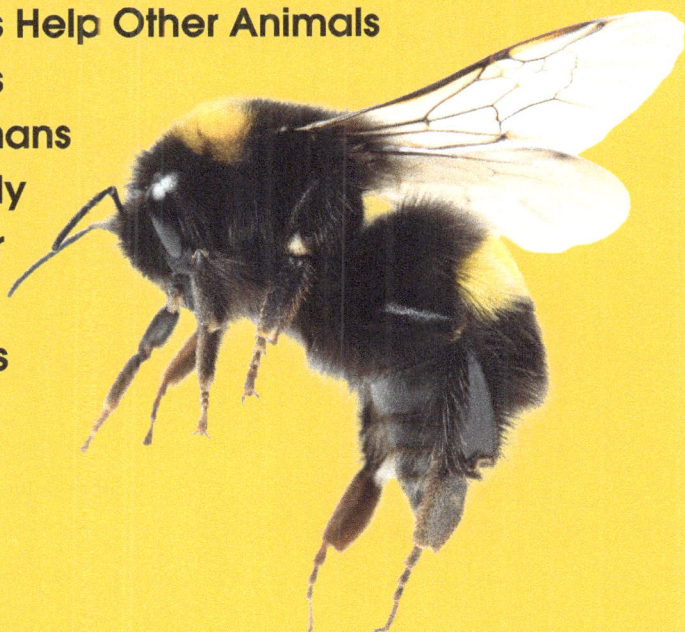

What Are Bees?

Bees are flying insects. An insect is a small animal without a backbone.

An insect's skeleton is on the outside of its body.

What Do Bees Look Like?

Bees have fuzzy hair on their bodies. They are mostly black and yellow.

Bees have six legs. They use their front legs to clean their head.

Bees have four wings. These wings make a buzzing sound when bees fly.

Female bees have a stinger. Male bees do not have a stinger.

Where Do Bees Live?

Bees live in large groups called colonies. These colonies live in nests called hives.

Most beehives are home to about 60,000 bees.

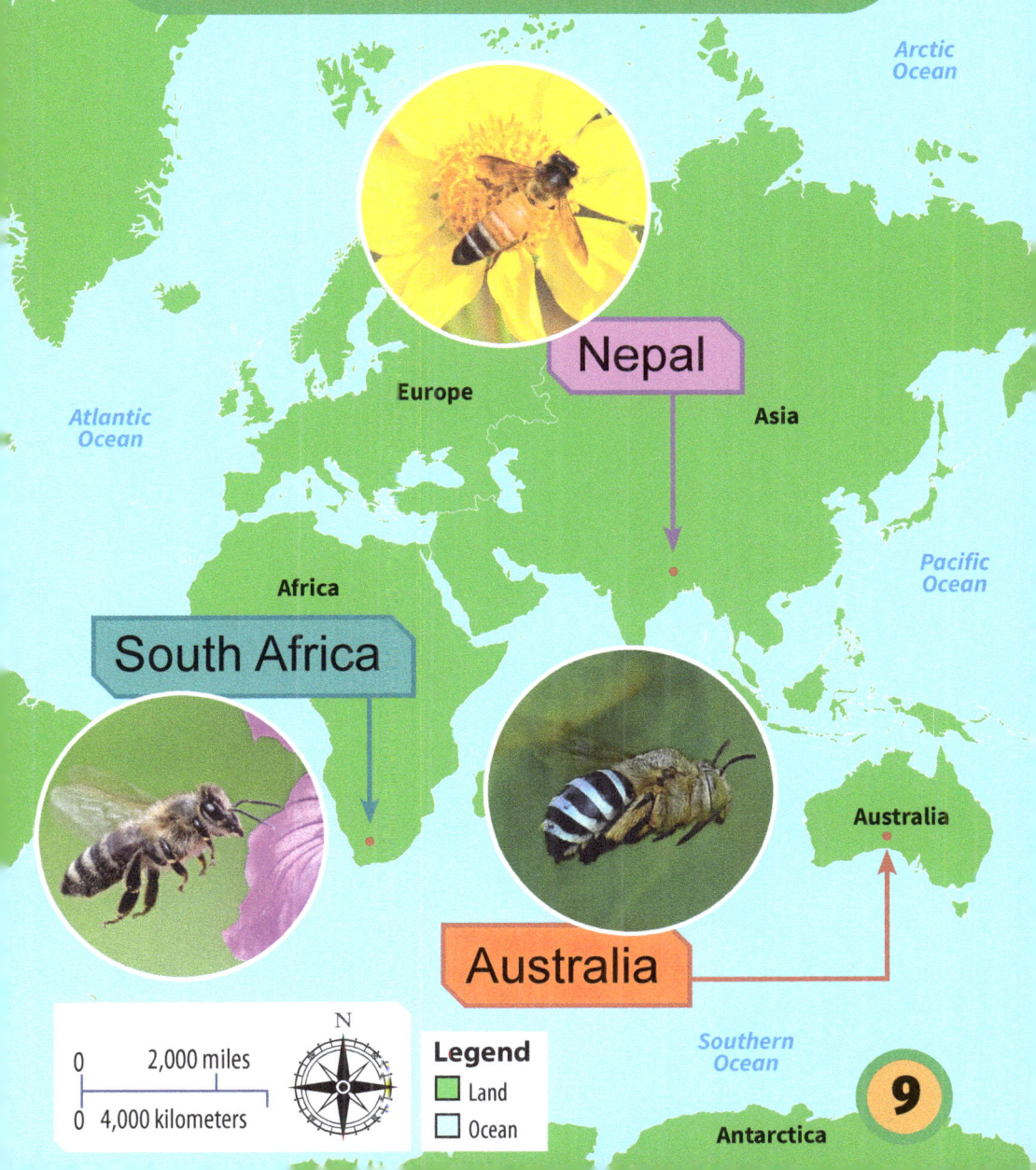

Bees live in every part of the world. Blue banded bees come from Australia. Cape honey bees live in South Africa. Rock honey bees are mainly found in Nepal.

Arctic Ocean

Nepal

Europe

Asia

Atlantic Ocean

Pacific Ocean

South Africa

Africa

Australia

Australia

Southern Ocean

0   2,000 miles
0   4,000 kilometers

N

Legend
☐ Land
☐ Ocean

Antarctica

9

What Do Bees Eat?

Bees eat pollen and nectar from flowers. Pollen is a kind of fine powder that flowers make. Nectar is a kind of sweet liquid flowers make.

Bees have a special tongue that works like a straw. This lets them drink water and nectar.

How Do Bees Talk to Each Other?

Bees talk to each other using special smells. These smells are called pheromones.

Bees have wires on their heads called antennae. They use their antennae to smell pheromones.

Bee Life Cycle

Bees have four stages in their life cycle. These stages are egg, larva, pupa, and adult. Queen bees lay all the eggs in a hive. The eggs hatch into larva after about 3 days.

Larvae grow for about 6 to 9 days.

Larvae turn into pupae. They hide inside hard shells called cocoons. All of their body parts grow at this time.

Pupae become adults after about 21 days. Adult bees have different jobs. Worker bees gather food. Drone bees help the queen bee make more eggs.

Curious Facts About Bees

Bees can fly up to 20 miles (32 kilometers) per hour.

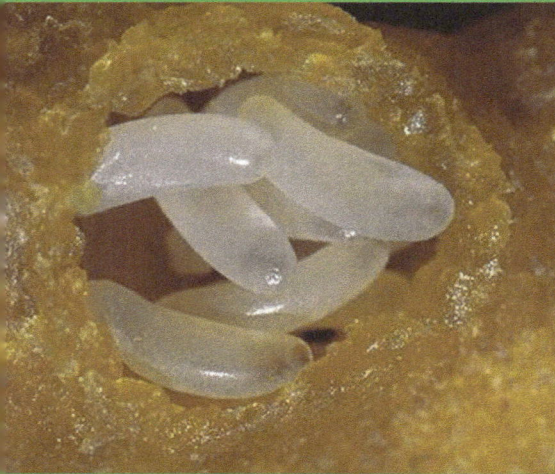

Queen bees lay around 1,500 eggs per day.

A bee can use its two front feet to taste things.

Most bees visit 50 to 100 flowers before they go back to the hive.

It takes about 12 bees their entire lives to make just one teaspoon of honey.

A bee's wings flap between 12,000 and 15,000 times each minute.

17

Kinds of Bees

There are more than 20,000 different kinds of bees. Honeybees, bumblebees, carpenter bees, and killer bees are some of the most common.

Killer bees are known to chase people if upset. They are not more dangerous than other bees.

Bumblebees have fuzzy black and yellow bodies.

Carpenter bees are mostly black. They make nesting holes in wood.

Honeybees are golden yellow. They have dark brown stripes.

How Bees Help Earth

Bees carry pollen from flower to flower. This pollen goes from the male parts of the flowers to the female parts of the flowers. This is called pollination.

Pollination helps plants make fruits and seeds. Fruits and seeds can grow into new plants. All of Earth's plants help to make air for life to survive.

How Bees Help Other Animals

Animals need plants to eat. Without bees, animals would be very hungry.

Bees pollinate some of the most delicious foods on Earth. There would be less nuts, chocolate, and honey without bees.

How Bees Help Humans

Bees make honey. Honey is very good for people to eat. It can help keep your body healthy.

Bumblebees only make a small amount of honey. They eat this honey themselves. Honeybees make enough honey for themselves and people to eat.

Bees in Danger

Bees around the world are disappearing. Scientists think climate change is one reason this is happening.

Climate change is when a hot place gets cooler, or a cool place gets hotter.

Special chemicals called pesticides can get rid of weeds. Farmers use pesticides to protect their crops.

Pesticides are very dangerous to bees. Bees around the world are dying from pesticides.

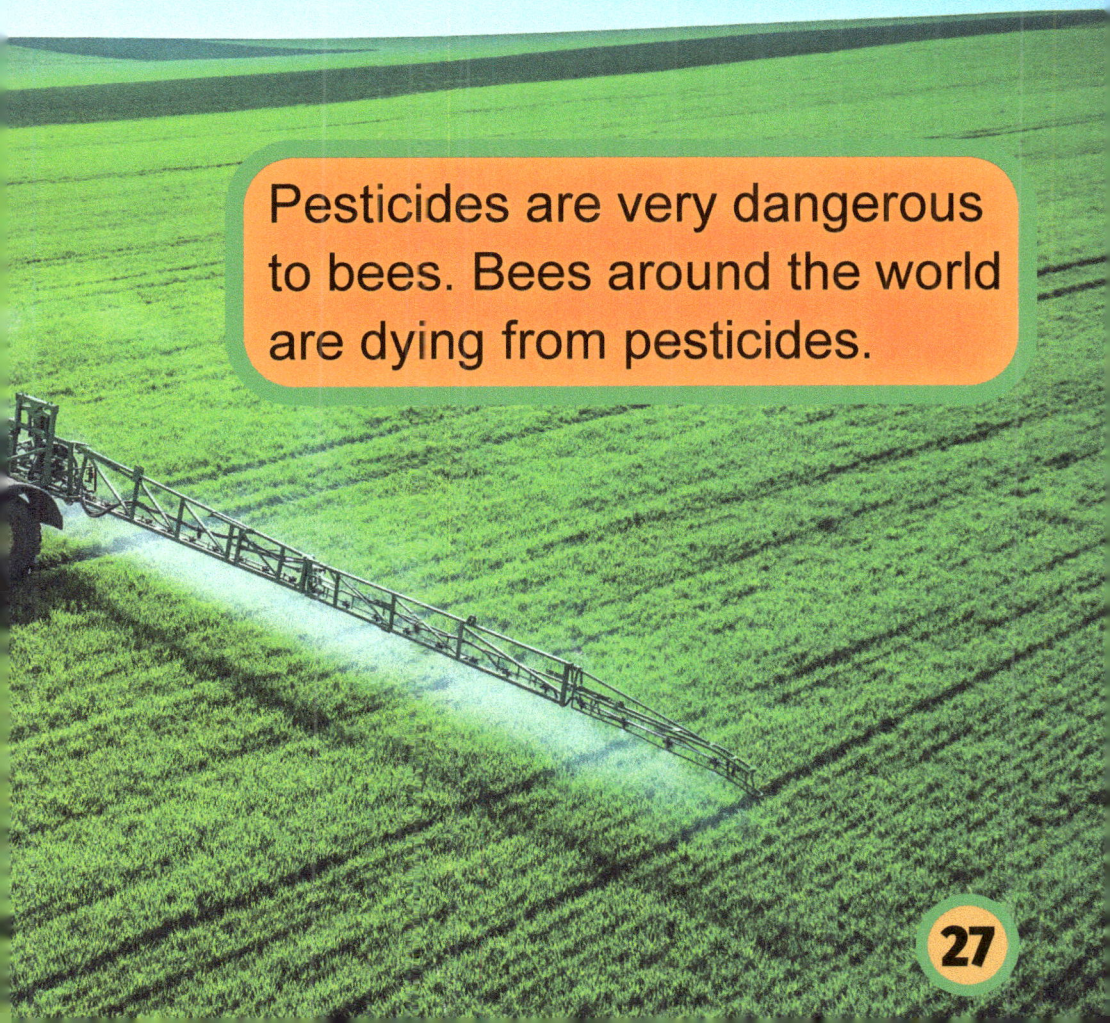

How To Help Bees

People can plant flowers that have a large amount of nectar in them. Bees like lavender, lilacs, and sunflowers.

You can make a "bee hotel" out of wood. This will attract bees to your garden. Bee hotels can keep bees safe and help their numbers grow.

People can help bees by spraying their weeds with vinegar instead of chemicals.

Quiz

Test your knowledge of bees by answering the following questions. The questions are based on what you have read in this book. The answers are listed on the bottom of the next page.

1 How many legs do bees have?

2 What are the wires on a bee's head called?

3 What do killer bees do if they are upset?

4 What food do bees make?

5 What is climate change?

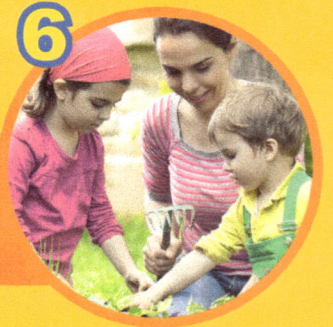

6 What flowers do bees like?

Explore other books in the Animals That Make a Difference series.

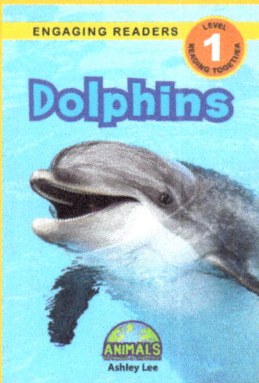

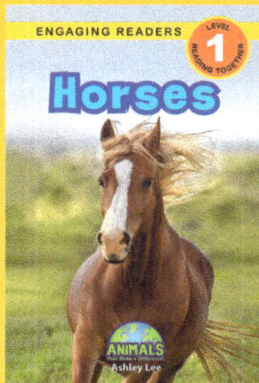

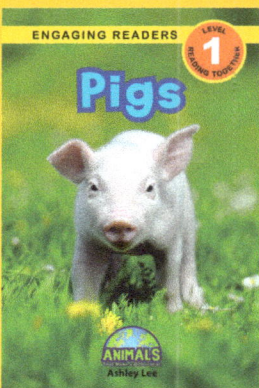

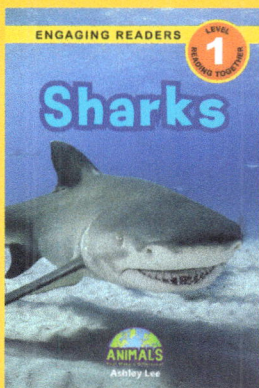

Visit www.engagebooks.com to explore more Engaging Readers.

Answers:
1. Six 2. Antennae 3. Chase people 4. Honey 5. When a hot place gets cooler, or a cool place gets hotter 6. Lavender, lilacs, and sunflowers

www.ingramcontent.com/pod-product-compliance
Lightning Source LLC
Chambersburg PA
CBHW051235020426
42331CB00016B/3379